THE SECRET TE
OF SUCCESSFUL

How To Become The Next Successful Woman In Your

Life And Business

AMOO E. OLAMIDE

Table of Contents

INTRODUCTION

In the last 10 years, the way women think about and relate to their careers has changed dramatically. According to the National Partnership for Women and Families, 93 percent of women are now employed, and 80 percent of these women are now in leadership positions. But there's a catch: the way we define success has changed. Today's leaders are not only more diverse—they are also more likely to be women. This is changing the face of corporate America, as women bring more knowledge and experience to the workplace. In order to better understand how successful women think about their career, I've spent the last few years interviewing hundreds of women across all walks of life and across all industries.

CHAPTER 1

The Secret Thoughts of Successful Women

Have you ever wondered why some people seem to succeed while others fail? Most people would say it's because of their hard work and determination. However, they are wrong. The truth is that there is something special about successful women that separates them from other women. These women have some secret thoughts that separate them from others. This secret thought is what separates these women from others. They think differently. For example, successful women tend to be better at solving problems than other women.

Successful Women Think Differently When it comes to solving problems, successful women are often more creative than other women. Successful women also think differently than other women. When a successful woman thinks differently, she can solve problems in new and creative ways. Successful women can do this because they can think outside the box. A box is a very limited way of thinking. It is a box that only allows you to think within certain boundaries. A box limits your creativity. If you want to develop creativity, you need to stop thinking within a box. The first step in developing creativity is to learn to think outside the box. If you want to learn how to think outside the box, you should start by reading books on creativity.

Books on creativity will teach you how to think outside the box. You can also try practicing the techniques from these books. What Are Some Techniques for Thinking Outside the Box? Here are some techniques for thinking outside the box:

1. Find Something New To Do You may not be able to develop creative ideas when you are in a time crunch. This is why it is important to find something new to do when you are running out of ideas. You can find something new to do by taking a walk, going for a drive, or doing some other activity that you have never done before. When you take a walk, you may find that you have an idea that you want to try. If you are on a walk, you may want to stop at a park and look around. You may notice a place that you would like to go. This could be a restaurant, a museum, or even a park. If you are driving, you may see something that you want to stop and look at. If you are doing something that you have not done before, you may find yourself thinking about how you can do it

differently next time. You may be able to get ideas from looking at things in a different way.

2. Create a Scenario You may be able to come up with creative ideas when you are creating a scenario. You can use this technique when you are writing, or when you are thinking about your problem. When you are creating a scenario, you may think of things that you have never thought of before. You may think of things that you have never done before. If you are writing, you can write down some ideas that you have. You may find that you can come up with some ideas by doing this.

3. Find Something That Is Already Out There You may be able to come up with creative ideas when you find something that is already out there. You

may be able to come up with ideas for something that is already out there.

A lot of people have this notion that success is easy, but it is actually quite difficult. If you are really serious about reaching the top, you'll have to put in a lot of effort. You can't expect to reach the top overnight. The most successful people will tell you that they worked really hard for their success. If you want to be successful, you should work as hard as you can to achieve your goal. Your success depends on how hard you are willing to work and how much you put into it.

Reference

In our world, women are often held back by their expectations. They think that they have to be beautiful. They have to be thin. They have to be sexy. They have to be smart. And if they aren't, then they feel like failures.

They don't like themselves. They feel worthless. They feel as if they can't do anything. They feel like they are a burden to everyone. They are afraid of people judging them. They feel that they are nothing. They have low self-esteem. It's not surprising that many women are suffering.

It is important for you to understand that this isn't the way to live. No woman can achieve success if she feels that way. If you are unhappy with the way that you look, then you need to get rid of this self-image. You need to feel good about yourself. You need to be happy. If you are not happy, then you can't be successful. You will have no self-confidence. You can't be confident if you are not happy with yourself. It is very important for you to love yourself. This doesn't mean that you have to be perfect. Just know that you are a beautiful person and that you are special. If you do this, then you will be happy.

If There are many things you can do to be successful in life. One of them is to be self-motivated. If you don't work hard at your goals, it will never happen. The only way to be successful is if you keep trying hard. Remember that success doesn't just come overnight. You have to work on it every day. It takes a lot of time and effort. Your parents don't always tell you that, but they should. They may not always give you enough encouragement. They might have their own ideas about what you should do. But you are the one who has to do it, so don't listen to them.

STEP TO SUCCESS

The first step to success is to think about your problems before you begin working on them. This will help you to figure out how to tackle your problems. If you wait until you get into the middle of the problem, it is almost impossible to get things done and solve it. You have to know what is wrong before you start the solution. Once you know what is the problem, you can start fixing it. It's hard to solve a problem if you don't know what is the problem. Most problems take time to fix because they are complex and have lots of details to work on.

When you are working on solving a problem, you have to understand the problem. You also have to know what you are doing and how you are doing it. You should always be aware of the problems in your life. You will never succeed if you don't have enough information about your problems. You have to understand how you are going to solve your problems. This will help you to figure out what to do. You can do this by talking to others or by reading books. You need to know what you are doing before you do it. It's important to know what you are doing, so that you can fix the problems. You should think about the problems that you are facing. This will help you to get rid of the problems.

What women need to know is that it is not what you know; but who you know that counts. You can do well if you have the right connections and the right people around you. It is a big deal to get ahead. To succeed at work, you need to be connected to the right people. They need to trust and believe in you. You can make lots of connections through networking, but you must take the initiative and ask others for help. If you are not doing the right things, no one will do them for you. To be successful, you need to be assertive and confident. Don't be shy, or afraid to ask for what you need. If you know how to talk to people and are confident in yourself, you will go far. Being a good listener is also important.

A secret thought will guide you toward success if you read it every day. If you are able to figure out what you think about most of the time, then you can succeed in life. That is the reason why you should always think about what you want. When you are thinking about what you want, you will have a goal. Then you will be able to achieve your goals. It is important to always be motivated and to keep yourself motivated. To be motivated, you should focus on what you want and work hard to accomplish that. If you want to achieve a high level of success, you have to think about the things you need to do. You should be very positive and focused. The more positive and motivated you are, the higher the chances you'll have of succeeding in life.

To get the best from yourself and to reach your goals, you should think about your personality. Your personality will help you to succeed in life. A person with a positive personality is more likely to be successful. On the other hand, if you are negative and pessimistic, then you will have a hard time reaching your goals. To get the best from yourself and to succeed in life, you have to think about your strengths. You should not concentrate on your weaknesses. Instead, you should focus on your strengths. It is important to use all your resources, including your strengths, to achieve your goals. Your character will also help you to succeed in life. If you want to succeed in life, you should develop your character. You should always show that you are responsible. A person with responsibility is more likely to be successful. In the end, you will be able to make your own decisions and to decide for yourself. You should never give up if you are facing difficult times.

Summary

There is something special about successful women that separates them from other women. Successful women have secret thoughts that separate them from others. When a successful woman thinks differently, she can solve problems in new and creative ways. Read books on creativity to learn how to think outside the box. Take a walk, go for a drive, or try something that you have never done before.

You may be able to come up with creative ideas by looking around. You can use this technique when you are creating a scenario or thinking about your problem. If you are writing, you can put some ideas down in writing. If you want to be successful, you should work as hard as you can. Your success depends on how hard you are willing to work.

It is very important for you to love yourself. Just know that you are a beautiful person. If you do this, then you will be happy. There are many things you can do to be successful in life. One of them is to be self-motivated.

Remember that success doesn't just come overnight. You have to work on it every day, and it takes a lot of time and effort. What women need to know is that it is not what you know, but who you know that counts. You can do well if you have the right connections and the right people around you. Don't be shy or afraid to ask for what you need.

If you want to achieve a high level of success, you have to think about the things you need to do. To be motivated, you should focus on what you want and work hard to accomplish that. Your personality will also help you succeed in life.

CHAPTER 2

What Women Think and Feel About Success, Money, and Happiness

Being successful means being happy. A successful person is usually happy. Why is this? There are a lot of reasons why this is so. It's because being successful will give you many things that will bring you happiness. If you are not happy with the way your life is going, it will be hard for you to be successful.

The things that make you happy are usually the things that you get when you are successful. For example, when you are happy, you usually have money and nice things in your life. If you are successful, you will have lots of money and a lot of things in your life. These will make you happy. The people who are most successful and happy usually have a lot of money. They also have a lot of things in their life such as nice homes, good health, and nice cars.

The women who are successful and happy have usually worked very hard for their success. It is not easy to be happy. Many women want to be successful and happy. It takes a lot of work to be successful and happy. You have to be disciplined to be successful and happy. It takes effort to be successful and happy. Most of all, it takes a lot of luck. There are also a lot of things that can prevent you from being successful and happy.

1. You Have to Be Disciplined and happy. Discipline is the key to success. To be successful, you have to be disciplined. If you are not disciplined, then you will never be successful. It takes discipline to get to the top. It takes discipline to stay there. You have to have discipline in your life. It is not easy to be successful and happy.

Most of all, it takes a lot of luck. You have to be very disciplined if you want to be successful and happy.

2. You Have to Be Smart and smart people are successful. The best way to become successful is to be smart. If you are smart, then you will be successful. A smart person has the best chances of being successful. When you are smart, you are more likely to succeed. If you are not smart, then you have no chance of success. It is a matter of genetics. You cannot change your genetic makeup. What you can do is to change your habits. You have to study hard to get good grades in school. You have to work hard to achieve success in life.

Success is something that most people think they will never have. They think that when they grow up, they will be poor. But when it comes to money and happiness, most people think that they will be wealthy and happy.

However, the truth is that success, money, and happiness go together. You can't be rich without having success. You can't have success without being happy. You can't be happy without having a good income. This is why it's important to be a smart businesswoman. You need to work hard and study to become successful. That way, you can become wealthy and happy.

You need to be smart when you are thinking about becoming a business owner. Here are some tips that will help you to become successful as a business owner:

1. Know Your Goals When you are starting out, you need to know what your goals are. What do you want to accomplish with your business? Do you want to be successful? Do you want to make a lot of money? Do you want to become rich? Whatever your goals are, you need to make sure that you are

able to reach them. You can't be successful if you don't have a goal. So, you need to have goals before you start your business.

2. Be Organized You need to make sure that you are organized when you start your business.

3. You need to make sure that you are able to keep track of everything that is going on in your business. So, you need to be organized. When you are organized, you will be able to make sure that you are able to reach your goals.

4. Hire the Right People When you are starting out, you need to make sure that you hire the right people. You need to make sure that you are able to find good employees. You need to make sure that you are able to find people who are willing to work for you. You can't be successful if you don't have

good people working for you. So, you need to make sure that you are able to find people who will work for you.

5. Make Sure That You Get a Business Plan You need to make sure that you write down a business plan before you start your business.

6. A business plan will help you to know what you are doing and how you are going to do it. You can't be successful if you don't have a business plan. So, you need to make sure that you write down a business plan before you start your business.

7. keep your business budget in order. You need to make sure that you are able to get the right supplies. You need to make sure that you are able to pay your bills on time. You need to make sure that you are able to keep track of everything that is

going on with your business. When you are not organized, you will not be able to reach your goals.

8. Get Financial Advice When you are starting out, you need to make sure that you get financial advice. You need to make sure that you are able to pay your bills on time. You need to make sure that you are able to save money. You need to make sure that you are able to pay for things that you need. So, you need to make sure that you get financial advice before you start your business.

9. Make Sure That You Start Small When you are starting out, you need to make sure that you start small. You need to make sure that you are able to start small. If you don't start small, you will have a hard time making it.

10.Be Patient You need to make sure that you are patient when you are starting out. You need to be patient when you are learning how to do things. You need to be patient when you are trying to make changes in your business. If you are not patient, you will never be successful.

Many people think that success comes easily. The truth is that hard work is the key to success. Success comes when you learn to be responsible for your own life. You will have to take action to achieve your goals. You may also need to change some of your habits. You should try to be positive and optimistic. These are the two things that are most important to having a good life.

Summary

A successful person is usually happy. There are a lot of reasons why this is so. Being successful will give you many things that will bring you happiness. You have to be very disciplined if you want to be successful and happy. The best way to become successful is to be smart.

If you are not smart, then you have no chance of success. Knowing your goals and being organized are some tips that will help you become a successful businesswoman. The truth is that success, money, and happiness go together. When you are starting out, you need to make sure that you hire the right people. You can't be successful if you don't have good people working for you.

A business plan will help you to know what you are doing and how you are going to do it. When you are starting out, you need to make sure that you get financial advice. You need to be patient when you are learning how to do things. If you are not patient, you will never be successful at what you are trying to do in life.

How Successful Women Think About Money, Sex and More

Successful women think about money, sex and more. They always have a plan to take care of their financial future. They also know that if they don't take care of their health, it will be hard for them to be successful. There is no way they will be able to achieve their goals if they are not healthy and well. In fact, they will be able to keep up with their goals and reach for the stars if they have a good relationship with their partner. They know that a healthy relationship is the best one they can ever have. If they don't have a healthy relationship, it is very difficult for them to stay happy and positive.

When it comes to sex and money, I feel that we all want to be successful. We should work hard at making more money. We also want to have a successful relationship. We want to live the life that we want. We don't want to settle for anything less.

The next thing is that we should save a lot of money because it is important for us to have a good life. We need to be able to enjoy ourselves every day. We can't just sit around doing nothing, and we don't want to waste our money on things that don't matter. Saving money is the best way to enjoy yourself.

You can also use the money that you have saved up for other things that you want. You can use it for something else that is more meaningful to you. It's not only fun to save your money, but it is also good for you. It can help you feel better about yourself. You'll feel like a real person when you have more money.

When it comes to money, women are really good at handling it. They will use their money to buy themselves things they want. It doesn't matter whether it is shoes or clothes. Men usually don't buy things for themselves because they are not interested in doing that. This is because men only think about sex and they don't have time to think about buying themselves a new pair of shoes. But women can think of many other things when they are having a discussion about money. The reason why successful women are good at handling money is because they are educated. Educated women are good with words. If you want to get ahead in life, you need to speak in a clear way and you need to be able to write well. So if you want to get rich, you need to learn how to handle money. You can do that by reading magazines and books. When you are having a conversation about money, you need to be well-informed.

Summary

Successful women think about money, sex, and more. They know that if they don't take care of their health, it will be hard for them to be successful. There is no way they will be able to achieve their goals if they are not healthy and well. It's fun to save your money, but it is also good for you. You'll feel like a real person when you have more money.

Successful women are good at handling money because they are educated. Women are good with words and can think of many other things when discussing money.

CHAPTER 3

What Makes Women Successful

There are many things that make women successful, but the main reason is that they work hard. They have the determination to achieve success in their lives and to do everything that it takes to become successful. As a matter of fact, women who are successful have goals that they are working hard to reach. In other words, they know what they want and they are determined to achieve that goal. Also, successful women don't just sit around and wait for something to happen. They get up and go for what they want. They put in a lot of time, effort and dedication to achieve success.

Women are successful because they know what it takes to be successful. The first thing that you need to do is to know what you want to be. If you don't know what you want to be, then you won't be able to be successful. This is the hardest thing for many people to do, but it is the key to success. The second thing that you need to do is to work hard. The harder you work, the more likely you will be successful. The third thing that you need to do is to be optimistic. Being optimistic is important because if you are pessimistic, then you will not accomplish anything. It's a good idea to keep your mind positive because being negative can lead you to fail in life. If you keep your mind positive, then you can be happy and achieve your goals.

A lot of people think that women are better at being nurturing and caring than men. This is not true. Men and women are both the same. They both have the same needs. We all want to be loved, respected, and appreciated. We all want to be seen and heard. The only difference between men and women is that we are stronger and more physically capable than men. If you want to be a success, you need to keep your head up high. Don't be ashamed or afraid to tell the world that you are a woman. When you do, you'll find that people will respect you.

The secret thoughts of successful women is that they have an optimistic mindset. They believe that they can achieve whatever they want, but their lives don't happen to them. They believe that anything is possible and they try to work hard to achieve what they want. They are determined to make their dreams come true, but they also understand that they cannot accomplish everything alone. They are open to new ideas and willing to learn from others. They keep a positive attitude and do not allow themselves to get discouraged.

They know that hard work pays off and they don't expect things to happen overnight. They are the kind of women who will tell you how much they appreciate you when you do something nice for them. They are also happy to help you in any way they can. They are loyal friends and they believe that loyalty is very important. They always have your back and will never betray you. They are smart and successful, but they know that it takes a lot of hard work to achieve success. Their optimism and positivity has helped them to achieve many things in their life, including having a successful career. They are able to balance work and family and they do not complain about their busy schedule.

The Secret Thoughts Of Successful Women: Why Smart Women Are Different

The secret thoughts of successful women are different from those of other women. In fact, they are the same as the thoughts of successful men. They only think differently. That's why you should focus on the way you think and not the way you look. You should change the way you think by focusing on the good things you have in your life and not the bad things that you don't have. You should focus on your ability to do what you want and not your looks. Your looks are superficial, but your thoughts are real. You can overcome the bad thoughts that you might be having by changing the way you think. You will see the changes in your attitude and in your way of thinking.

Successful women believe that they have a mission. They know that their purpose in life is to make their lives better and to make other people's lives better. Successful women think about making their lives better and not just getting money or possessions. A successful woman thinks about helping people and making their lives better. She thinks about making her life better and the lives of others better. Successful women think about how they can help other people and not just themselves. They know that if they help other people, then they are going to help themselves as well. A successful woman knows that she cannot give up on herself. She knows that she has a purpose in life and that purpose is to make her life better. A successful woman thinks about what she can do to help other people and to make their lives better. She thinks about how she can help others and about the things that she can do to make their lives better.

If you want to be successful, you will have to work hard. No one will help you to be successful. You will have to try your best to accomplish your goals. People will be impressed with your success. You need to be able to work your hardest to achieve your goals. There is a lot of competition in this world, and people will want to take you down. You should always strive to improve yourself. Never give up. The best way to succeed is to go after what you want, keep working on it, and never stop.

You need to start working now. If you wait until later, you will be too late. Do not waste time. You need to get started now. You will only have so much time to accomplish your goals. You need to do what you can, when you can. You need to make sure that you know exactly what you want to accomplish. Write down all of your goals. Make sure that you can accomplish them. You can set goals that are impossible. You will still have to try your best. You need to find a mentor who can help you to achieve your goals. You can learn a lot from someone who has been there and done that.

Smart women are different from the other women because they have a lot more things in their life than others. For example, they are much more likely to work in the area of their interests and also, they are usually better at looking after themselves. If you are smart, you have a goal in your mind and you will try to achieve it. Smart women are often ambitious and they know how to get what they want.

In this post, we are going to discuss some of the qualities of smart women that you should learn.

1.   Smart Women Are Good At Self-Care, Self-care is an important part of being a smart woman. Many women who are not smart take care of themselves because they don't know how to do so. You need to make sure that you are well-groomed, that you are eating healthy and that you are taking care of yourself.

You should be able to take care of yourself, even if you are busy.

2.   Smart Women Don't Need A Man To Be Happy If you are a smart woman, you will not need a man to be happy. If you want to be happy, you should be happy with yourself. Many women feel that they can't be happy without a man. This is a very bad attitude. Smart women are not going to settle for less than what they deserve.

If you don't want to settle for less, then why should you settle for less? Smart women can be independent and strong. They do not have to depend on a man to get their needs met. They are capable of taking care of themselves. If you are a smart woman, you should know that you can take care of yourself.

I'm not saying that smart women are better than others. However, they can easily get along with people. They know how to handle different situations and different kinds of people. They also know how to use their intelligence to their advantage. I was able to observe this while I was working with a woman I worked with at my job. She knew how to read the mood of the person she was dealing with. She knew how to deal with difficult people. That's why I admire her because she doesn't let other people push her around. She stands up for herself and fights back when someone tries to harm her. She is also very successful in her life.

There are many women in the world. Some are smart and others aren't. If you are interested in being a smart woman, you should work on your intelligence. You need to try to improve yourself by going to the library or the internet to learn things that you don't know.

Some women are smarter than others. There are many factors that help determine if a woman is smart or not. The first thing that determines if a woman is smart is the way she talks. For example, an average person might talk at a normal rate and get their point across. On the other hand, someone who is very smart will speak faster than everyone else and get their point across quicker and easier. This will make you feel as though you are being talked to, not the other way around. A woman who is very smart may be able to do this without any help from you. She may also be able to do this with a wide variety of people. It's because she knows what she is talking about and can quickly explain it to anyone. The next thing that determines if a woman is smart is her ability to read. Smart women have been able to read since they were little girls. They know how to use books and magazines to educate themselves on what's going on in the world. A woman who is smart will understand the importance of education and reading. She will also understand the importance of knowing what's going on in the world.

When you meet a woman who is smart, she has a lot to offer you. She will not only be able to share her ideas and opinions with you, but she will also be able to read your mind. You will be able to communicate with each other effortlessly. When a smart woman gets to know you, she will know what you are looking for. She will also know what you need to hear. She will be able to tell you what you want to hear because she is a very smart person. This is why smart women are attractive. They are very much aware of what they want and what their partners want. This makes them very attractive to men. Smart women are always in the know when it comes to things like the economy, politics, sports, and culture. They know how to navigate through life, and this makes them more attractive than other women.

Summary

The secret thoughts of successful women are the same as those of successful men. You should focus on your ability to do what you want, not your looks. A successful woman knows that she cannot give up on herself. The best way to succeed is to keep working on it, and never stop. Smart women are different from the other women because they have more things in their life than others.

Smart women are often ambitious and they know how to get what they want. If you are smart, you have a goal in your mind and you will try to achieve it. Smart women can be independent and strong. They do not have to depend on a man to get their needs met. They are capable of taking care of themselves.

If you are interested in being a smart woman, you should work on your intelligence by learning more about it. Some women are smarter than others. The way a woman talks determines if she is smart or not. Smart women are always in the know when it comes to things like the economy, politics, sports, and culture.

CHAPTER 4

The Secret Thoughts Of Successful Women, Part 1: The Power Of The Mindset

Many people say that when you start a new project, the first thing you need to do is to have a good mindset. If you think that you can do it, then you can probably do it. So, the mindset you start with will affect your success. You need to believe that you can achieve what you want. You need to have a positive mindset. In fact, many people say that mindset is the most important factor when you want to accomplish something in life. So, you must first build a strong mindset before you start anything else. You need to be persistent and confident in order to achieve your goals.

If you have a positive mindset, you will be able to keep going even if you fail or experience setbacks along the way. As an entrepreneur, you need to have a clear vision of where you want to go. You need to have a clear goal and you need to know how you will get there. If you have a clear goal, you can easily find ways to make it happen. But, if you don't have a goal or a vision, you will end up with nothing at the end of the day. As an entrepreneur, you should also learn from your failures and mistakes. Don't let them hold you back. Instead, use them as learning tools to grow and develop. The best way to achieve your goals is to first set a plan.

If you really want to succeed, then you can do it. Don't let other people tell you that you can't do it. If you believe that you can do it, then you will. You can't fail if you really try to do something. If you keep trying and trying, you'll eventually succeed. You'll see that you can do it. No one can stop you from doing this if you really want to succeed. No matter what others say, you should just keep going on and succeed. If you really want to succeed, then you can do it.

It's important for you to be positive all the time. We all face challenges in life, but if we are constantly negative about the things we have to do, then it's hard for us to achieve our goals. If you are having a bad day, it's a good idea to take a few minutes to think about all the things that are positive. Instead of focusing on your problems, you should focus on your strengths and your abilities. You should try to have a positive mindset. This will help you to overcome your obstacles.

You must have a certain mindset in order to succeed in life. A successful person is one who has learned how to deal with the situations in life and has also learned how to enjoy the success that he or she achieves. There are many books that you can read about success and motivation. You may also find useful information online. You can also visit your local library and look for any books that are related to the topic. If you don't have time to do this, you can just watch movies or television shows about the topic. You can watch any movie or television show that will help you learn about the topic.

You can find some good ones by browsing through the internet. There are also some websites that you can visit and read interesting articles about motivation. You need to realize that not all people are born to be successful. Success does not come automatically. You have to work hard in order to get it. In order to get success in life, you must learn how to deal with the problems in life. You need to know how to control your emotions so that you can concentrate on your goals. You need to be aware of the things that you need to do in order to achieve your goals. In order to get success, you need to think about the future. This means that you need to plan your future and make sure that you have the necessary skills for it. If you don't have enough skills, you need to get the necessary training.

If you are a fan of the TV series "The Office", then you should watch the episodes that are related to success. There are different types of success and failure. Some people may say that there is only one type of success, but it is not true. There are different types of success. For example, you can be successful at school, you can be successful at work, you can be successful in sports and you can be successful in your relationships with people. These are all types of success. Failure is different from success. Some people may say that there is only one type of failure, but it is not true. There are different types of failure. For example, you can be unsuccessful at school, you can be unsuccessful at work, you can be unsuccessful in sports and you can be unsuccessful in your relationships with people. These are all types of failure.

It's easy to give up when things don't work out for us. That is why it is good to have the right mindset so that you will be able to face challenges and get past them. You should always believe in yourself and your abilities. You shouldn't let anyone tell you that you aren't good enough. Instead, you should keep working hard and believe in yourself because only then will you accomplish great things. People who succeed in life are those who do the most they can do, no matter what. They keep at it and don't give up. They believe in themselves and they believe in their dreams. They believe that anything is possible if they work hard enough. Their mindset is one of success. If you want to change your mindset, you need to think about the reasons why you want to change your mindset. You can begin by telling yourself that you will change your mindset. You should also remind yourself that you have made a commitment to your self-improvement. It will not be easy to change your mindset but you have to try your best. You will feel a little bit of discomfort but this is a necessary part of your process. You have to overcome your fear of failure and try to be optimistic.

It is important to keep yourself motivated every day. You can use positive affirmations when it comes to motivating yourself. Positive affirmations are words that help you feel good about yourself. It is important to think positively all the time and focus on what you like and what motivates you. You should always keep a positive mindset about yourself. This way, you will succeed in achieving your goals. You can achieve many things in life by simply keeping your mind positive and focused on what you like.

Here are some positive affirmations that you can use when it comes to motivation:

1.   I am the best. I am the best at everything I do. There is no one who is better than me. I am the best student. I am the best friend. I am the best athlete. I am the best singer. I am the best cook. I am the best dancer. I am the best at being me.

2.   I have nothing to prove to anyone. I don't need to prove myself to anyone because I already am the best at what I do. I don't need to show off or impress anyone with my accomplishments. I am enough just as I am. I am good enough.

3.   I am worth it. I am worth whatever I put my mind to. I am worth more than any amount of money and fame or recognition. I am worthy of every success that I earn and every success that I achieve. I am worth it all.

4.   I am worth it. I am worth the fight. I am worth the pain. I am worth the struggle. I am worth the effort. I am worth the sacrifice. I am worth it all.

5.   I am worthy of happiness. I deserve happiness. I am worthy of joy. I deserve joy. I deserve love. I deserve to be loved.

10 Lessons On How To Succeed As A Woman In Business

There are many ways to succeed as a woman in business. If you have a good idea, you should always work on it and improve on it. That's how you will earn success. It is a good idea to seek help from people who know more about business. Ask them for advice. Get feedback from them and take it as a learning experience. Always work hard on your ideas. If you don't, you won't succeed.

Women are great entrepreneurs and excellent business owners, They have been around for thousands of years. They have survived through difficult times. So, women have lots of experiences that they can share with other women. Women also have a lot of different talents and skills. That means that a woman has many ways of helping others and making them feel special. One thing is for sure: women have a great impact on society. They are the ones who bring life into the world. That is why it is important to learn how to be successful in business, because women are great in any field. Here are some lessons that will help you succeed in business.

1.   The first thing that you need to do when starting a business is to think about how you can promote yourself.

2.   You should keep in mind that your first customers will be your family and friends. They are the ones who can help you grow your business.

3.   If you want to be a success, you need to know how to do your homework and research well.

4.   You should always be willing to take a risk. That means that you must be willing to give up your comfort zone. This is very important if you want to have a successful business.

5.   You should work hard and stay positive.

Being a woman is not easy. There are many challenges you have to face. It is important to learn how to overcome those challenges.

1. Be Realistic It is very important to be realistic when it comes to your dreams and goals. You have to set goals that are achievable and you need to stay focused on achieving them.

2. If you don't set goals that you can achieve, then you will never reach your goals.

3. Don't Let Other People Hold You Back When you are in business, you need to know how to let go of other people's opinions. You need to make sure that you only focus on your own business and not on what other people think. This is a very important lesson that you should learn.

4. Be Confident and Determined A good leader has to be confident and determined. When you have these two traits, you will be able to do a lot of things.

5. You Need To Know How to Handle Tough Times. Tougher times are inevitable in any business. You have to know how to deal with them.

6. You Need To Understand That Money Is Not Everything. Having money is not the only thing that makes you successful. It is important to have other important qualities as well.

7. Be Your True Self Don't try to act like someone else. Be yourself. If you try to act like someone else, then you will not be able to achieve your goals.

8. Take Good Care of Yoursel Taking care of your health is very important. If you don't take care of your health, then you will not be able to achieve your goals.

9. If you are thinking about starting your own business, then you are probably already busy working on

it. You should also be very careful to get the most out of your business.

Rules Successful Women Live By

A successful woman is someone who follows rules. She knows how to get things done. The rules help her to become a better person and to be a great role model. The best way to achieve success is to keep on improving yourself. The best thing you can do is to set goals and set out to accomplish them. You can also work on yourself to be a better person. This will help you achieve your goals.

You should always be prepared to do well in everything that you do. You should think of ways to improve yourself. You can improve your physical appearance by eating healthy foods. You can also improve your mental capabilities by reading good books. In fact, you can improve many things about yourself. You don't have to wait for your time to do this. You can take the initiative and make your life more successful.

There are lots of different rules that successful women follow. Many people think that being successful requires a lot of money, but that's not true. Some of the rules that successful women follow include:

1.   They work very hard.

2.   They always give their best effort.

3.   They always try to be cheerful.

4.   They always maintain a good relationship with their family and friends.

5.   They always try to do things for others.

6.   They never allow themselves to be distracted by unimportant things.

7. They always keep their word.

8. They always treat people with respect.

9. They always have a clear vision.

10. They always pay attention to detail.

11. They always follow the rules.

12. They always follow their own sense of value.

13. They always work towards their goals.

14. They always follow the path of righteousness.

15. They always choose their career wisely.

16. They always act on what they feel in their heart.

17. They always take time out to relax.

18. They always know how to balance work and family.

Conclusion

In conclusion, the key to success in anything is this: you must have a vision for what you want to accomplish. It must be so clear in your mind that it is almost impossible to mistake it for anything else. If you do, you will surely fail. Successful people live their lives as if they have already achieved the goals they have set for themselves. They don't waste time wondering what might happen if they didn't get there. Instead, they work toward the goal.

Printed by BoD™in Norderstedt, Germany